Wall Paintings

Nathaniel Harris

PowerKiDS press.

New York

Published in 2009 by The Rosen Publishing Group Inc.
29 East 21st Street, New York, NY 10010

First Edition

Senior Editor: Claire Shanahan
Designer: Rachel Hamdi/Holly Fulbrook
Project Maker: Anna-Marie d'Cruz
Models: Shannon O' Leary, Ross Zavros
Photographer: Andy Crawford

Library of Congress Cataloging-in-Publication Data

Harris, Nathaniel, 1937-
  Wall paintings / Nathaniel Harris. — 1st ed.
    p. cm. — (Stories in art)
  Includes index.
  ISBN 978-1-4042-4440-5 (library binding)
 1. Mural painting and decoration—Juvenile literature. 2. Mural painting and decoration—
Technique—Juvenile literature. I. Title.
  ND2550.H35 2009
  751.7'3—dc22
                                    2007052739

Title page, p16/17: The meeting of Antony (ca. 82–30 BC) and Cleopatra (51–30 BC) 1747–50 (fresco) by
Tiepolo, Giovanni Battista (Giambattista) (1696–1770), Palazzo Labia, Venice, Italy/Alinari/The Bridgeman
Art Library; p6: © Hubert Stadler/Corbis; p7: Portrait of a young girl (fresco), (first century AD), Museo e
Gallerie Nazionali di Capodimonte, Naples, Italy/Lauros/Giraudon/The Bridgeman Art Library; p8: School
of Athens, detail of the center showing Plato and Aristotle with students including Michelangelo and
Diogenes, 1510–11 (fresco) (detail from 472) by Raphael (Raffaello Sanzio of Urbino) (1483–1520), Vatican
Museums and Galleries, Vatican City, Italy/The Bridgeman Art Library; p9: Shah Abbas I (1588–1629) and
a Courtier (detail) (fresco) by Persian School, Chehel Sotun, or The 40 Columns, Isfahan,
Iran/Giraudon/The Bridgeman Art Library; p10/11: Ay performing the opening of the mouth ceremony on
the mummy of Tutankhamun (ca. 1370–1352 BC) from the Tomb of Tutankhamun,
New Kingdom (wall painting) by Egyptian, Eighteenth Dynasty (ca. 1567–1320 BC), Valley of the Kings,
Thebes, Egypt/The Bridgeman Art Library; p12/13, front cover: The Betrayal of Christ, ca. 1305 (fresco)
by Giotto di Bondone (ca. 1266–1337), Scrovegni (Arena) Chapel, Padua, Italy/The Bridgeman Art
Library,p14/15: © Banco de Mexico, Diego Rivera & Frida Kahlo Museums Trust, Mexico D.F./DACS,
London; p18/19: © Oliver Strewe/Corbis; p20/21: Joe Fox/Alamy.

Manufactured in China

Contents

What are wall paintings?

Wall paintings are pictures that have been painted directly on the surfaces of walls. They are different from pictures simply hung on walls, which can be moved at any time. Wall paintings become a permanent part of a house or site. They are also known as **murals**, from the Latin word for "wall."

The earliest surviving paintings were done about 34,000 years ago, on the walls of caves and on rocks used as shelters by wandering groups of people. The earliest paintings of all were probably hand stencils, made by placing a hand against a rock and blowing or flinging powdered color at it. When the hand was removed, its shape could still be seen inside the surrounding color (see the illustration below). Stone Age artists in Europe went on to produce superbly lifelike animal paintings, working deep in caves. Some peoples, such as Australia's **Aborigines**, have continued to make rock paintings until very recent times (page 18). When people began to build houses, palaces, and places of worship, they decorated many walls and ceilings with painted images. For centuries, such murals were the most important type of picture.

◀ Stencilled hands and other paintings cover the walls of the Cave of the Hands in the province of Santa Cruz, Argentina. Some of these images are 9,000 years old. Many rock paintings discovered in Europe are even older, dating from as long ago as 25,000 years earlier.

Great wall paintings were created by the ancient Egyptians (see page 10), the Greeks and Romans (see right), the Maya of Central America, and the great civilizations of Asia (see page 9).

A strong Christian tradition of murals developed in Europe, and especially Italy. There, artists such as Giotto (see page 12), Michelangelo, and Raphael (see page 8) pioneered a great new movement, the Renaissance. Later, murals made a powerful impact in the hands of modern masters, such as Diego Rivera (see page 14).

Not all murals are the work of professional artists. People sometimes paint the outsides of their houses for traditional or political reasons (see page 20). And there are also paintings done on public surfaces without permission, known as graffiti. Usually spray-painted, these range from scribbles to skillful works of art.

▲ *Lost in thought, a girl wonders what she should write. This Roman mural dates from the first century AD. Originally in Pompeii, it is now in the National Museum, Naples, Italy.*

How to use this book

Background information on each wall painting featured, including its creator, date, location, and history

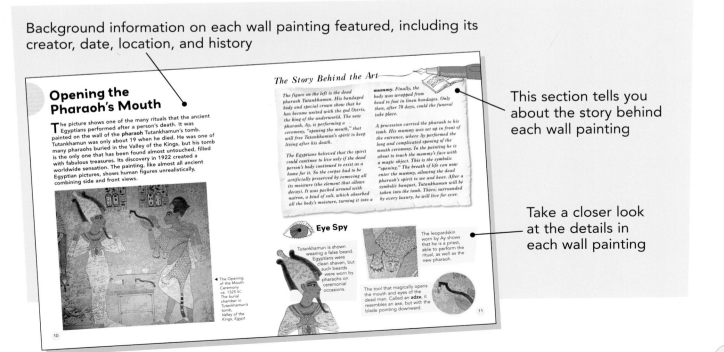

This section tells you about the story behind each wall painting

Take a closer look at the details in each wall painting

How are wall paintings made?

Until modern times, all the colors used in painting were made from natural sources, such as minerals and plants. These paint colors are called **pigments**, which are ground into a powder and then mixed with a substance to make them fluid. Such a substance is called a **medium**. Egg, oil, and wax are among the mediums used in making paint. Prehistoric painters are believed to have used water or animal fat as a medium. They used shells for holding their colors, and probably made their brushes from animal hair tied to sticks.

The most common mural technique has involved spreading a layer of plaster on the wall before painting. This is done to create a surface that will be smooth and will also absorb the paint. **Medieval** Italian artists, such as Giotto, developed an effective technique that they called *fresco* ("fresh"). They used water-based colors to paint on newly made plaster while it was still slightly damp. As the plaster and paint dried, chemical changes fused them into a single substance, so that the paint was no longer likely to fall off from its plaster base.

▲ The School of Athens is an imaginary group portrait of ancient Greek philosophers. It was painted in 1511 by the Italian Renaissance artist Raphael, and it is now in the Vatican Museum, Rome.

▶ This beautiful seventeenth-century Persian painting shows King Abbas II being served by a courtier. It belongs to a group of murals in a pleasure pavilion, the Palace of Forty Pillars, built for the Persian kings at Isfahan in Iran.

Artists who painted frescoes had to work quickly. A new section of wet plaster was laid on the wall each working day, and all of it had to be painted before the plaster dried out. Artists developed methods of rapidly transferring outline drawings onto the plaster. For large-scale projects, scaffolding had to be put up so that the artist could reach every part of the surface. Most artists employed teams of assistants. As well as working quickly, the artist often had to create a picture that could be seen and understood from a distance or from below. For both of these reasons, most frescoes are bold and colorful paintings in which detail is less important than impact.

Many Italian frescoes are still in good condition, but those in the damper atmosphere of northern countries tended to decay. This was one reason for the development of oil painting—painting done on canvas that uses oil instead of water as a medium. Oil paintings may be large or small. Many were and are intended to hang on a wall. But in recent times, oil paintings on very large canvases have also been made as murals, to be permanently attached to the wall or ceiling.

Opening the Pharaoh's Mouth

The picture shows one of the many rituals that the ancient Egyptians performed after a person's death. It was painted on the wall of the **pharaoh** Tutankhamun's tomb. Tutankhamun was only about 19 when he died. He was one of many pharaohs buried in the Valley of the Kings, but his tomb is the only one that has been found almost untouched, filled with fabulous treasures. Its discovery in 1922 created a worldwide sensation. The painting, like almost all ancient Egyptian pictures, shows human figures unrealistically, combining side and front views.

◄ The Opening of the Mouth Ceremony ca. 1325 *BC The burial chamber in Tutankhamun's tomb, Valley of the Kings, Egypt*

The Story Behind the Art

The figure on the left is the dead pharaoh Tutankhamun. His bandaged body and special crown show that he has become united with the god Osiris, the king of the underworld. The new pharaoh, Ay, is performing a ceremony, "opening the mouth," that will free Tutankhamun's spirit to keep living after his death.

The Egyptians believed that the spirit could continue to live only if the dead person's body continued to exist as a home for it. So the corpse had to be artificially preserved by removing all its moisture (the element that allows decay). It was packed around with natron, a kind of salt, which absorbed all the body's moisture, turning it into a **mummy**. Finally, the body was wrapped from head to foot in linen bandages. Only then, after 70 days, could the funeral take place.

A procession carried the pharaoh to his tomb. His mummy was set up in front of the entrance, where Ay performed the long and complicated opening of the mouth ceremony. In the painting he is about to touch the mummy's face with a magic object. This is the symbolic "opening." The breath of life can now enter the mummy, allowing the dead pharaoh's spirit to see and hear. After a symbolic banquet, Tutankhamun will be taken into the tomb. There, surrounded by every luxury, he will live for ever.

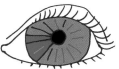 **Eye Spy**

Tutankhamun is shown wearing a false beard. Egyptians were clean shaven, but such beards were worn by pharaohs on ceremonial occasions.

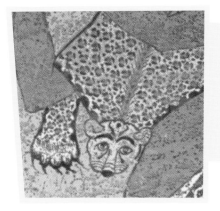

The leopardskin worn by Ay shows that he is a priest, able to perform the ritual, as well as the new pharaoh.

The tool that magically opens the mouth and eyes of the dead man. Called an **adze**, it resembles an axe, but with the blade pointing downward.

The Betrayal of Christ

This work is by a medieval Italian artist, Giotto di Bondone (1267–1337). It is part of a series of 39 large frescoes, painted around 1305 in the Arena Chapel (also known as the Scrovegni Chapel) in Padua, Northern Italy. The subject, the life of Jesus Christ and his ancestors, had been painted many times before. But Giotto made these religious scenes much more human and dramatic than earlier artists had done, though he still shows the holiest figures with large golden **haloes** around their heads. Giotto was the first great painter of a new era in history, the Renaissance ("rebirth"), which later produced such famous artists as Leonardo da Vinci, Michelangelo, and Raphael.

◄ The Betrayal of Christ
*Giotto di Bondone
ca. 1305
Arena Chapel,
Padua, Italy*

The Story Behind the Art

*Jesus of Nazareth has come to Jerusalem, accompanied by his 12 **disciples**. His religious teachings have angered the people in power, who wish to arrest him. They get their chance when one of Jesus' disciples, Judas Iscariot, decides to betray him.*

Giotto's painting shows the treacherous way in which Judas picks Jesus out—he embraces and kisses Jesus, just as a loyal disciple would do. The embrace is a signal to the soldiers that Jesus is the man they are looking for. They are already closing in, forming a ring around Jesus and Judas. Behind them (to the left), there is confusion. One man is trying to run away but is being held back by a sinister hooded figure. Jesus' hot-tempered disciple Peter is trying to fight back and has sliced off the ear of one of the attackers. To the right, one of Jesus' enemies is pointing at him as if ordering his arrest. Jesus himself is calm and serious. He already knows that his mission will involve suffering and death.

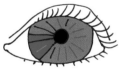

Eye Spy

A moment after Judas has kissed Jesus, they look each other in the face. They are unmoving figures in a scene full of movement. Judas' robe almost envelopes Jesus, but Jesus' haloed head dominates the composition.

Jesus' disciple Peter strikes out at one of his master's enemies. Like Jesus, Peter is shown with a haloed head to indicate his holiness.

The night sky is filled with torches, staffs and spears, a club, and even a horn. Crisscrossing and spread out, these add to the sense of drama and movement.

The Arrival of Cortes

The Mexican artist Diego Rivera (1886–1957) painted this crowded and action-packed mural. The *Arrival of Cortes* describes a major historical episode. After Christopher Columbus's famous voyages to the New World, Europeans began to conquer and settle the Americas. In 1519, a Spanish force led by Hernan Cortes reached Mexico. It overthrew the ruling Aztec empire and made Mexico a Spanish colony. Rivera's painting is not really about Cortes' arrival, but about what the Spanish did to Mexico and its peoples. Rivera's view of events is one-sided, since he does not show the cruelties of the **Aztecs**. But his terrible picture of oppression and injustice makes a tremendous impact.

▼ The Arrival
of Cortes
*Diego Rivera
1951
National
Palace, Mexico
City, Mexico*

The Story Behind the Art

Rivera's painting tells many stories, all of them parts of one big story about the impact of the Spanish invaders on the Aztecs and other Mexican peoples. It is filled with episodes in which the Spanish enslave or kill the Mexicans and take their land. The Spanish leader, Cortes, is shown in the central group at the front of the picture. Rivera makes Cortes pale and sickly, possibly to remind viewers of the deadly diseases that Europeans brought with them to the Americas. Here, Cortes is being paid by a fellow-Spaniard for the right to own Mexican land and receive **tribute** from the inhabitants; an official makes a record of the deal.

Many other episodes show the sufferings of the conquered people. Spanish soldiers brand a Mexican slave. Natives work under the whip, yoked to a plow like beasts, carrying logs, and mining to enrich their Spanish masters. The Spanish are dominant figures equipped with armor, firearms, and horses. All of these were previously unknown in Mexico, like the cattle and other domestic animals that the Spanish are also bringing into their newly conquered land.

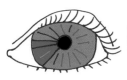 **Eye Spy**

An African watches a Spanish soldier branding a Mexican. The African is also a slave, one of millions who will be brought to the Americas over the centuries.

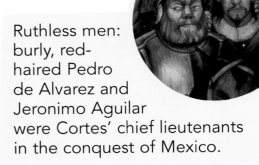

Ruthless men: burly, red-haired Pedro de Alvarez and Jeronimo Aguilar were Cortes' chief lieutenants in the conquest of Mexico.

These Mexicans have been yoked together like horses or oxen and set to pull a plow. Another Mexican drives the plow, supervised by a whip-wielding Spaniard.

Antony and Cleopatra

The painter of this picture was the Italian artist Giambattista Tiepolo (1696–1770). Tiepolo was famous for his murals. He worked on large-scale projects in Italy, Germany, and Russia, covering the walls and ceilings of palaces and churches with crowded, colorful scenes. During his lifetime, people were fond of pictures that looked like episodes from a play or opera. So Tiepolo's figures are grandly posed within a painted, theater-style frame of columns and arches that look as if they are real. In fact, all the architecture in the picture is painted, including the front steps that seem to lead toward us. Paintings that look completely real are described as **trompe l'oeil** (French for "deceive the eye").

▶ The Meeting of Antony and Cleopatra
Giambattista Tiepolo
1747–50
Labia Palace, Venice, Italy

The Story Behind the Art

It is 42 BC. Mark Antony is a renowned soldier and one of the most powerful men in the Roman Empire, ruling all its eastern provinces. Cleopatra is the queen of Egypt, but she can only keep her throne while the Romans trust her. To find out whether she is loyal to Rome, Antony has ordered her to come to him at Tarsus, a city in Turkey.

The painting shows their meeting. Cleopatra has arrived in a magnificent state barge, accompanied by a host of followers and slaves. The wealth and splendor of Egypt are on show. Cleopatra's beauty has overwhelmed Antony. Instead of commanding her as he expected, he is already falling in love with her as he leads her into the palace.

Antony and Cleopatra are probably the world's most famous lovers. They married and ruled the East together. But Antony's fellow-Romans disliked seeing him dominated by an Egyptian woman. When he and Cleopatra had children, Antony made them kings and queens of provinces he controlled. Obviously, he was no longer working for Rome. In 31 BC, Octavian, the ruler of the western Roman Empire, went to war with Antony and Cleopatra. The following year, they lost a great sea battle at Actium. As Octavian advanced, the doomed lovers took their own lives, giving their story a nobly tragic ending.

Eye Spy

Cleopatra's ship carries a large carved figure of **Neptune**, god of the sea. Those who sail in the ship hope the **figurehead** will protect them. Neptune appears as a half-human, half-fishy being.

The figure with a turban emphasizes the eastern setting of the painting. Humbly crouching, he is probably a servant of the great queen.

The greyhound is a Tiepolo "trademark," found in many of his paintings. The artist always shows the dog as an elegant, sensitive, and intelligent-looking creature.

Spirits Among the Rocks

Aboriginal peoples have lived in Australia for at least 40,000 years. Before European settlers arrived just over two centuries ago, the Aborigines survived by moving from place to place, hunting and gathering their food. They built no permanent homes, but used cliffs and overhanging boulders as shelters. Many rocks and shelters became sacred ceremonial places, and Aboriginal artists painted and engraved images on them. Used again and again over thousands of years, the surfaces became crowded with images of spirits, humans, animals, reptiles, birds, fish, and many other objects. Thousands of sites have survived and new ones are still being found.

▶ *A Quinkan and other figures*
Date unknown
Part of a rock surface in the Giant Horse Shelter, near Laura, Queensland, Australia

The Story Behind the Art

The dominant figure in the picture is a humanlike creature with outstretched arms. Its long body and limbs, and its staring eyes, identify it as a spirit of the dead called a **Quinkan**. Behind it stands another, smaller Quinkan. Hidden away among rocks, Quinkans were said to come out in the dark, lurking just out of sight of campfires. There are different versions of what they were like, but all agree that they were frightening and dangerous. They could change shape at will, and people lured away by them were turned into **zombies**. Quinkans were particularly unfriendly toward strangers. The white figure with the twisted leg below the Quinkan may be one of its victims. Perhaps it is one of the Europeans who oppressed the Aborigines, magically avenged.

If so, the white figure, like the horse's head on the left edge, is much later than some other parts of the picture. Many rock paintings combine relatively recent images of modern objects with ancient pictures of, for example, long-extinct animals. Similarly, supernatural ancestors and spirits may appear beside everyday images. Here, among other things, the Quinkan is accompanied by humans, a bird, a **stingray**, a horse's head, and a sea cucumber!

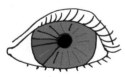 **Eye Spy**

The horse's head is a modern touch. Horses were brought to Australia by Europeans, so this must have been painted in relatively recent times.

The figure appears to have fallen. It may be a victim of the Quinkan, or it is possibly linked with the figures to its left, which look as though they are fighting.

This is a stingray, a flat fish with a barbed, poisonous tail. Fish and other marine creatures often feature in Aborigine paintings.

The Easter Rising

This mural has been painted on the side of a house in Northern Ireland. It salutes the memory of a famous Irish rebellion, the 1916 **Easter Rising** against British rule. Murals of this kind have been seen frequently in Northern Ireland. They are not just about the past. Northern Ireland is a province of the United Kingdom, separate from the Irish Republic. The province has been bitterly divided between people who want to keep their link with Britain and those who would like Northern Ireland to become part of the republic. Murals on both sides picture moments in their history that they are proud of. A mural like this one, glorifying the Easter Rising, shows that the people who live in the house are republicans. The orange, white, and green bands are the colors of the Irish Republic; the main scene is a copy of a painting showing the rebel defense of the Dublin General Post Office, the center of the rising.

▼ *Easter Rising mural*
Date unknown
On the side of a house,
Ardoyne, Belfast,
Northern Ireland

The Story Behind the Art

The scene shows the rebels holding out against the besieging British Army. They are in the main hall of the General Post Office (GPO) in the middle of Dublin, the Irish capital. This large building was the headquarters of the rising, seized by the rebels on April 24, 1916. From the GPO, they boldly proclaimed an Irish republic, independent of Britain, while they also occupied other places in the city. But there were only about 1,600 rebels, and when British troops arrived in force, the rising had no chance of success. The rebels' aim was to hold out long enough to set a heroic example and win support for future risings.

The picture shows the situation after several days of fighting. The military commander of the rebels, James Connolly, lies wounded, his ankle shattered, but he continues to issue orders. The other rebel leader, Patrick Pearse, stands nearby, a revolver in his hand. A British shell or **incendiary bomb** has started a fire. The end is only hours away.

The following morning, the rebels managed to evacuate the building. But they soon realized that further resistance was useless. On August 29, they surrendered to the British. Pearse, Connolly, and other rebels were executed as traitors. That only made them heroes to most Irish people, and started a chain of events that led to the creation of the Republic of Ireland.

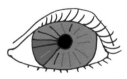

Eye Spy

Soldiers defending one of the windows fire down the enemy forces.

A nurse and a Catholic priest look after a dying man.

A rebel soldier uses a hose in an attempt to control the fire started by a British shell or bomb.

Design a graffiti poster

What you do:

1 Take a look at the kind of writing, symbols, **tags**, and illustrations used in graffiti in your local area. You can also use the Internet for research and study different designs of the printed letters used in magazines and newspapers.

You will need:
letter-sized paper
• colored pencils, chalks, pastels, and felt-tip pens
• large construction paper •
colored marker pens
• selection of newspapers, magazines, and graffiti type
• double-sided tape or thumbtacks

2 Brainstorm on paper. Think of all the different words that you could graffiti—consider what subjects you like in school, what you like to do in your spare time, what kind of food you like to eat, what makes you happy or sad, and so on. If you're working with a friend or classmate, why not discuss each other's lists to give you ideas?

3 Using your research, experiment with different styles of lettering and various materials to write on the paper. Try to incorporate an illustration or tag with the word so that they work together. For example, you could fill the spaces between letters and add graffiti "accessories," such as crowns, arrows, haloes, or shadows to the letters. Your graffiti statement should be easily readable, but it's important to have fun with it and play with the words and tags.

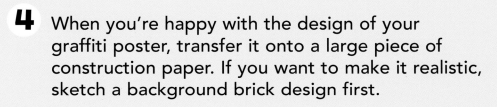

4 When you're happy with the design of your graffiti poster, transfer it onto a large piece of construction paper. If you want to make it realistic, sketch a background brick design first.

5 Attach the construction paper to a wall, using double-sided tape or thumbtacks. If you are working with friends or classmates, ask an adult if you can use a whole wall to place your graffiti posters together.

You could make the graffiti poster part of a graffiti mood wall, an area dedicated to you and your favorite things, rather than just one statement piece.

Create a mural

This is a large-scale mural based on a famous work of art that you can make with friends or classmates.

You will need:

tabloid-sized paper
• images of famous works of art • ruler
• pencil • paints, chalks, and marker pens
• paintbrush
• magnifying glass

What you do:

1 From the Internet, print out a color copy of a famous work of art or use a color photocopy from a book.

When choosing which artwork to use, think about the materials and technique used by the original artist, since you will need to imitate these for a true result. For instance, Van Gogh used large paint strokes in his *Starry Night* painting.

2 Draw horizontal and vertical lines to create a grid of nine squares on the work of art. If you're working with friends or classmates, you will take a square each to work on.

Top Tip! Use a fine pen pencil when making your g so the lines do cover much of artwork.

3 When you have decided which square of the grid you are going to recreate, study the square carefully. Consider the size and positioning of the different details in the square and how they relate to one another.

Top Tip! Use a magnifying glass if you want to have a close look at the square.

4 Lightly sketch the outline in pencil on a tabloid sheet. Try to recreate the size and positioning of each detail in your square to fill the page.

5 When you're happy with your outline, start painting, again copying the colors and shading in the square.

6 When you and your friends have all the finished squares, put them together and the edges should match up to make one big picture.

Make a fresco

What you do:

1 Cut the burlap to letter size. Place the burlap on top of a piece of corrugated or strong cardboard to protect the table from wet plaster, and to allow you to move it easily later on.

2 Mix the plaster of Paris according to the instructions on the pack.

3 Pour the plaster of Paris in the center of the burlap square. Using a spoon, spread it out in a thin layer from the middle into a rectangular shape, so that no burlap is visible underneath the plaster. Leave about 1/2 in. (1 cm) of burlap around the edge. Allow the plaster to dry for an hour or more.

4 While the plaster is drying, plan and design your sketch on paper.

Top Tip!
Gently shake the sides of the cardboard to get rid of any air bubbles in the plaster of Paris.

5 Use sandpaper to gently smooth out any bumps or sharp edges in the plaster.

6 Lightly dampen the plaster with a wet sponge. This will help the watercolor paints soak into the plaster.

7 With watercolor paints, draw and color in your design on the re-dampened plaster.

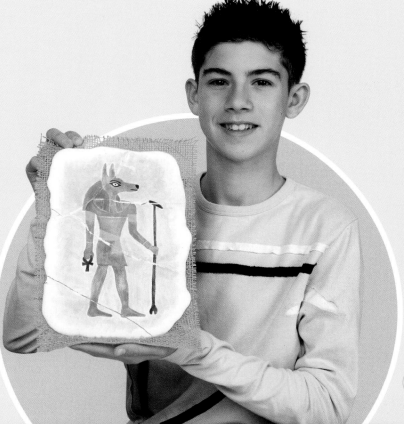

8 When you have finished coloring and the plaster is dry, make the fresco look like a centuries-old work by bending it in your hands to create chips and breaks in it. Don't worry about the plaster falling off the burlap—it has stuck to it as it dried.

9 Seal the plaster with a thin layer of glue, allowing it to seep into the cracks.

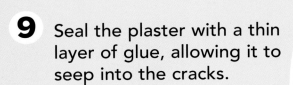

Glossary

Aborigines The people who inhabited Australia before Europeans arrived. The adjective is Aboriginal.

adze Tool like an axe, but with a blade pointing downward, at right angles to the shaft.

Aztecs The people who dominated most of Mexico from about 1450 AD until the Spanish arrived in 1519 AD.

disciples Followers of a religious teacher.

Easter Rising 1916 Irish Rebellion against British rule.

figurehead The carved human or other figures frequently placed on the prow (front) of a ship.

fresco Italian word meaning "fresh." It describes the technique of painting on fresh, still damp plaster.

halo An artistic symbol in the form of a circle of light or a golden disk, above or around the head of a holy or divine person.

incendiary bomb A bomb designed to start a fire when it hits its target.

medieval Describes anything to do with the Middle Ages (about 500–1500 AD).

medium Oil, water, or any other substance used to make pigment (see below) into paint.

mummy A dead body, preserved by the removal of all its moisture. This has been done by humans, but sometimes also occurs naturally.

mural A wall painting.

Neptune Roman sea god.

pharaoh A king of ancient Egypt.

pigments The colors used in painting in their dry form, before they are mixed with a medium (see above).

Quinkans In Australian Aboriginal belief, frightening spirits of the dead.

stingray A flat fish with a barbed, poisonous tail.

tags Used in graffiti to describe a person's chosen nickname or personally designed signature.

tribute Money or goods paid to a dominant power or individual.

trompe l'oeil A French term meaning "deceive the eye." It describes paintings so lifelike that viewers may believe they are looking at real creatures or objects.

zombies Imaginary humans without minds or souls, found in many myths and stories.

Find out more

Books to read

Aboriginal Art of Australia: Exploring Cultural Traditions by Carol Finlay (Lerner, 1999)
Diego Rivera by Joanne Mattern (Checkerboard, 2005)
Giotto and Medieval Art by Lucia Corrain (Peter Bedrick, 2001)
The Life and Work of Michelangelo Buonarroti by Richard Tames (Heinemann, 2006)
Painting Murals: Images, Ideas, Techniques by Patricia Seligman (North Light, 1988)
Prehistoric Art by Susie Hodge (Heinemann, 1997)
Stencils and Screens by Susie O'Reilly (Thomson Learning, 1994)
The Usborne Book of Stencil Fun by Ray Gibson (EDC Publishing, 1996)
Trompe L'Oeil: Creating Decorative Illusions with Paint by Roberta Gordon-Smith (David & Charles, 1997)
What Makes a Raphael a Raphael? by Richard Mühlberger (Bt Bound, 1999)

Websites to visit

Due to the changing nature of Internet links, PowerKids Press has developed an online list of Web sites related to the subject of this book. This site is updated regularly. Please use this link to access this list:
www.powerkidslinks.com/sia/wpaint

Places to go

The Art Institute of Chicago, Chicago, has a collection of Trompe L'Oeil artwork.

The Metropolitan Museum of Art, New York, has a permanent collection of Ancient Roman and Italian Renaissance frescos, including works by Michelangelo Buonarrito. It also has a permanent collection of prehistoric art.

The Museum of Modern Art, New York, has a permanent collection of Diego Rivera artwork.

Index

Photos or pictures are shown below in bold, **like this**.